Introduction

SCHOOL: YOU MAY LOVE IT OR loathe it, but you can't escape it. It wasn't always like this. Free school that you must go to is quite a new idea. Just 150 years ago, learning was costly. Few parents could afford it. Instead of studying, kids worked.

Sounds great? Not when you learn that "work" was climbing up chimneys or down mines, or picking caterpillars off crops all day. For kids that did these jobs, going to school was a distant dream. It was a dream that would release them from lives of poverty and grinding labour.

Those kids who did get an education were mostly boys. Girls didn't count, let alone add and subtract. Schools taught boys reading and writing – and perhaps fighting and riding, too. Those who wouldn't study were beaten until they did. Some fought back, often with loaded guns and razor-sharp swords! If this sounds very different from your own school, it was. Education can be wilder and weirder than you could possibly imagine. Turn the page, and find out more!

Learning for Life

WHAT IS YOUR FAVOURITE LESSON? How about walking through a steamy rainforest learning which plants are good for healing or food? Maybe you'd prefer to train as a sword-swinging warrior? Lessons like these don't sound much like school but, in different times and places, they are what children learned. Education means learning what you need to know for life, whether it's fighting or computers.

● ●

This book is mostly about schools, but remember that until very recently few children ever stepped inside a schoolhouse. Instead, their families taught them valuable skills and ancient traditions. In many places this still happens: "school" is a shady tree, or a rocking canoe.

Would You Believe . . . ?

Polynesian fishing school
On the tiny Pacific island of Pukapuka, "education" used to mean going fishing. Boys learned from their fathers the names of the fishes and where each was found. There is a school now, but fish hooks are still as important as school books.

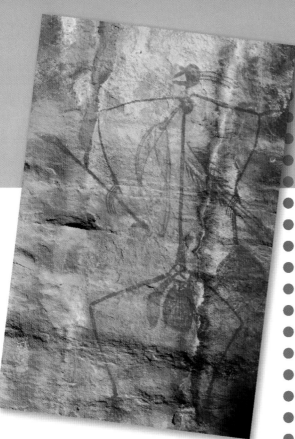

Girls and boys

In the past, learning for life usually meant boys and girls studying different things. For when they became adults, men and women usually led very different lives. As these examples from 16th-century Aztec Mexico show, parents trained their sons and daughters in different – but equally useful – skills.

Aztec girls ▼
Women in Mexico led hard lives of housework and grinding maize. Mothers punished disobedient daughters with lungfuls of stinging smoke from a chilli fire.

Australian hunter ▲
In ancient Australia, there was no written language and hardly any words for numbers. Without writing and arithmetic to learn, lessons were very different from those today. Education meant imitating rock paintings of hunts (above) and other outback survival skills.

Storyteller by Joe Cajero Jr, a Native American artist

Aztec boys ▲
Fathers taught their sons to be tough. They also taught them how to fish, carry loads and paddle canoes. In one way at least, their education was similar to girls. Naughty boys suffered the same chilli fire punishment.

Cave School

Would You Believe . . . ?

Tiny tunnellers
Rarely, archaeologists find evidence that prehistoric children learned new skills. In an ancient copper mine in Wales, some tunnels are too small for an adult to squeeze in. Parents must have taught their children to mine ore they could not reach themselves.

WITH WRITING still many centuries in the future, the Stone Age schoolgirl never had to learn to spell "woolly mammoth". Learning to avoid its shiny tusks, on the other hand, was a useful skill that ensured a longer life. Besides survival skills like dodging mammoths, we can only guess at what else Stone Age children learned in their cave classrooms; lessons leave no fossils.

We can be sure that parents taught their children practical skills. They would have taught them to identify, gather and prepare food plants. Children may have even hunted on their own: archaeologists in North America have found stone spear and arrow points made to fit child-size weapons.

Hunting mammoths ▼
Neanderthal people, who thrived in Europe and Asia 100,000 years ago, taught their children how to help hunt mammoths. Children probably learned to cut off escape routes and shake bushes to drive the huge hairy beasts towards adult hunters.

A mammoth skeleton found in Los Angeles, USA

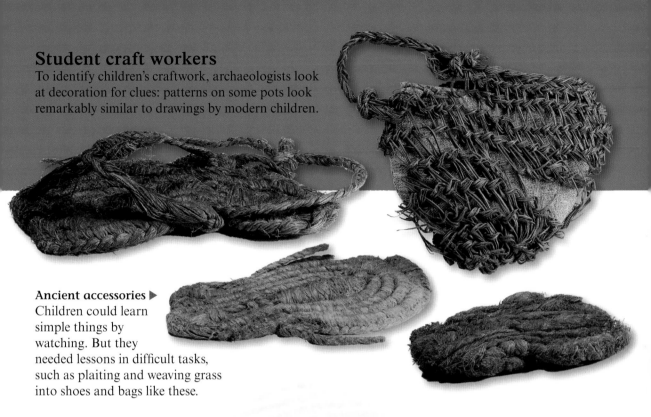

Student craft workers

To identify children's craftwork, archaeologists look at decoration for clues: patterns on some pots look remarkably similar to drawings by modern children.

Ancient accessories ▶
Children could learn simple things by watching. But they needed lessons in difficult tasks, such as plaiting and weaving grass into shoes and bags like these.

There was no time for childhood. If a family was to survive, children had to learn adult skills fast

Shepherds and farmers ▲
In Neolithic times, about 5,000 years ago, children learned new things. People gradually gave up hunting and looking for food, and began farming. Children were taught to help. They could herd animals and drive away predators, such as wolves. And they cared for crops by scaring birds or picking off insect pests.

Children's prints ▲
Children make mistakes, but just because an ancient pot is wonky it doesn't mean it was made by a child. Some clay artefacts have been found with tiny fingerprints made up of closely spaced lines. Only children could have left these.

A Day at the Gymnasium

I N ANCIENT GREECE, "A DAY AT THE gym" was a work-out for the brain as well as the body. Gymnasiums were colleges for older boys. They began as athletic training schools where Greek boys exercised without clothes. (The Greek word *gymnos* means "naked".) But by the 4th century BCE they also had schoolrooms and libraries. To prepare for the gymnasium, boys from wealthy families began studying from the age of seven.

Boys started by learning, reading, writing and arithmetic. Later they studied poetry and music. The slaves who took the children to school also helped in class. Roman children were also commonly taught at home by slaves – usually Greeks.

Scribe's tomb ▲
The wax tablets on which children learned to write were not just for school. They were used by adults too. This Roman scribe holds several tablets in his hand.

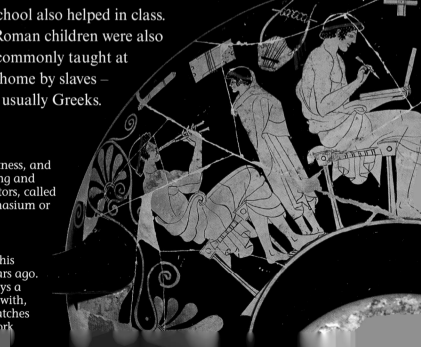

Boxing boys ▲
The Greeks admired physical fitness, and boys' education included fighting and athletics. Physical education tutors, called *paidotribes*, taught at the gymnasium or the *palaistra* (wrestling school).

Music school ▶
Greek painter Douris recorded this busy school on a vase 2,500 years ago. On the left, a music teacher plays a flute for his pupil to sing along with, and in the middle, a student watches while his teacher corrects his work.

Spelling it wrong

Teachers in Greek schools were often foreigners with poor knowledge of written Greek: archaeologists have found 2,500-year-old school slates with misspelled words for pupils to copy.

Words in wax ▶

Greek and Roman children wrote on a thin wax sheet stuck to folding wooden boards. The stylus that they used to scratch the words was pointed at the writing end; the other, flat end was an eraser.

Would You Believe . . . ?

Love your teacher

Greek doctor Hippocrates told his pupils to make this promise: "I will hold my teacher equal to my parents ... and think of his family as my own brothers. I will make him a partner in my work ... and share my money with him when he's penniless."

From about 50 BCE, Roman parents were packing off their sons and daughters to schools. The schools were often very basic. Pupils studied in rented rooms, or even in open shops with just a curtain to shut out the noise and dust of the street.

Lashings of discipline

Badly paid and overworked, Roman teachers often beat their unfortunate students as punishment for laziness or disobedience – or just to encourage them. The poet Martial, who lived near a school, complained, "You cursed schoolmaster, what right have you got to disturb us before the cock crows with your savage threats and beatings?"

Greek thinker Aristotle admired brutal teachers. He wrote: "All learning is painful."

Squire and Page

CLASHING NOISILY ON huge war-horses, armoured knights were the glamorous stars of medieval tournaments. In the watching crowd, the loudest cheers came from their schoolboy attendants: the teenage squires who prepared them for battle, and younger pages who ran errands. One day these castle scholars hoped to ride into battle too.

Pater noster qui es in caelis ·:·
Sanctificetur nomen tuum ·:·
Adveniat regnum tuum ·:·
Fiat voluntas tuas sicut in
caelo et in terra ·:· Panem
nostrum quotidianum da nobis
hodie ·:· Et dimitte nobis de-
bita nostra sicut et nos dim-
ittimus debitoribus nostris ·:·
Et ne nos inducas in temp-
tatione ·:· Sed libera nos
a malo ·:· Amen ·:·

◄ **Hornbook**
Children learned from a hornbook: a thin layer of horn protected the writing on the parchment.

For the sons of wealthy families, schooling began at the age of seven. Their parents sent them to study in the castles of relatives. Taught by priests, boys learned religion, and reading and writing in English, French and Latin.

Learn with Mum ▲
Parents who could read began teaching their children as soon as they were three or four years old. As well as the hornbook shown here, mothers used prayer books to teach reading.

● ● ● ● ● ● ● ● ● ● ● ●

"Manners books" told children that, at meals, they should spit politely on the floor – not rudely over the table

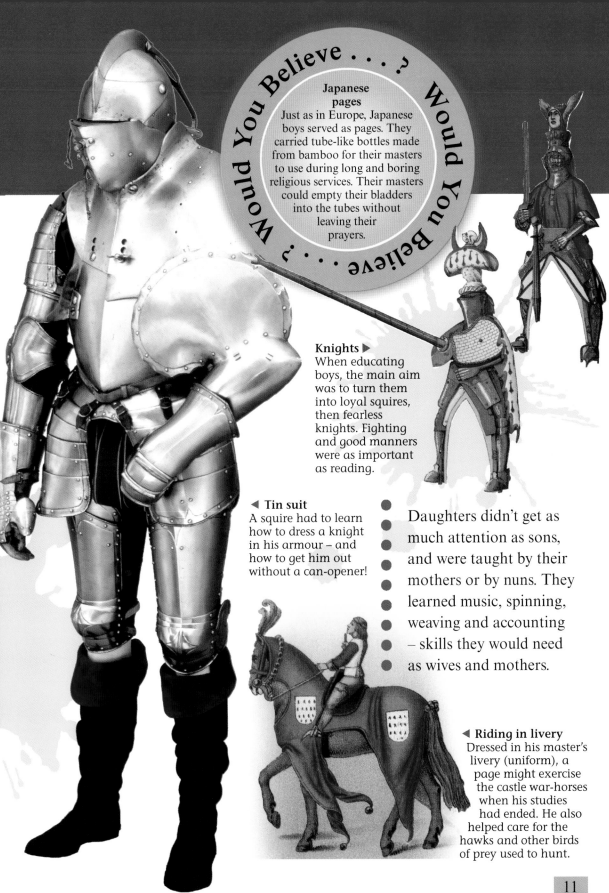

Japanese pages
Just as in Europe, Japanese boys served as pages. They carried tube-like bottles made from bamboo for their masters to use during long and boring religious services. Their masters could empty their bladders into the tubes without leaving their prayers.

Knights ▶
When educating boys, the main aim was to turn them into loyal squires, then fearless knights. Fighting and good manners were as important as reading.

◀ Tin suit
A squire had to learn how to dress a knight in his armour – and how to get him out without a can-opener!

Daughters didn't get as much attention as sons, and were taught by their mothers or by nuns. They learned music, spinning, weaving and accounting – skills they would need as wives and mothers.

◀ Riding in livery
Dressed in his master's livery (uniform), a page might exercise the castle war-horses when his studies had ended. He also helped care for the hawks and other birds of prey used to hunt.

Church and School

EDUCATION AND RELIGION are age-old partners. For people without reading skills, holy books, such as the Bible, are just meaningless piles of paper. So by teaching reading, religious people kept their faith alive. Writing skills were vital too, because, until the 15th-century invention of printing, all books had to be copied out in handwriting.

In Europe, the Christian church started the first schools to train priests and monks, in the 6th century. Based in monasteries and cathedrals, they taught pupils the words of the Bible. Mosques were the centre of education in the Muslim world.

300-year-old Turkish Koran

Illuminated pupil ▲
This illuminated (illustrated) letter "N" from a medieval book shows a student nun. When her studies were complete, she would have hand-copied books like the one in which she appears.

▼ Studying the Koran
Scholars of the Koran, the Muslim holy book, taught boys to memorise its verses by heart. Reading the book was less important. Promising students went on to study at a *madrasah*. In the Arab world today, the name *madrasah* refers to any kind of school, but traditionally it meant a college for older boys.

Some students joining 7th-century monasteries were so keen to learn, they waited outside for five days

12

At first, the Christian church schools in Europe taught pupils to read and write in Latin – the language in which the Bible was written. Only later did pupils study in their own language.

LA VILLE DE SOISSON

Reading and religion ▲
Missionaries, such as St Crispin (above), spread reading and writing skills along with knowledge of the Bible. The missionary message has not always been welcome. Early missionaries sometimes destroyed traditional beliefs and ways of life.

...? Would You Believe...? Would You Believe...? Would You Believe...?

Early universities
The world's first university, the University of Karueein in Fez, Morocco, was founded in 859 CE as part of a mosque. Europe's first university, at Bologna in Italy, began two centuries later, and Britain's first began at Oxford a century after that.

◄ **Novice monk**
Buddhism began in India in the 4th or 5th century BCE, and Buddhist missionaries spread the religion throughout Asia. Early Buddhist monks moved from place to place. Later, they set up permanent monasteries that became learning centres. The tradition continues today: this young monk is studying in Bhutan in South Asia.

13

Learning to Fight

Martial arts ▼
Many ordinary schools teach martial (fighting) arts, not for war but as a fun way to keep fit.

I MAGINE A DAY AT school that went: 8.30, assembly; 8.45, unarmed self-defence; 9.30, maths; 10.15, weapons training. For students at war schools, this was a typical timetable, because in more warlike times, fighting skills were as important as writing and arithmetic.

Of all warrior students, Spartan boys of ancient Greece had the harshest lives. They left home for military school aged seven. They were starved, given few clothes and whipped. Their training was so tough that when they went to war it felt like a holiday.

Viking swords ▶
Viking boys learned to fight at the age of five. Twelve-year-olds were considered to be men and able to fight alongside them. As teenagers, they might become military leaders.

Would You Believe . . . ? Would You Believe . . . ?

Whipping exams
At the annual festival of Artemis-Orthia, Spartan boys endured a "whipping examination". *Mastigophori* (whip-carriers) beat them severely while their parents encouraged them to endure the pain without crying out. Some boys died from the ordeal.

Yanomami warriors ▲
The Yanomami people of South America have a warlike tradition. Children learn about warfare through play-fighting. They paint themselves with battle colours and endure ferocious piercings. Hunting teaches them marksmanship.

Mexico's Aztec people also trained their sons as fighters. Noble boys studied at a warrior school called a *calmecac*. Their first taste of war was as a bag- or weapon-carrier. They then fought "flowery wars" – battle-games in which enemy prisoners were sacrificed.

School for officers ▲
Since the 18th century, military academies, such as Paris's *Ecole Polytechnique*, have trained officers to lead their countries' armies. Today, the tradition of educating disciplined leaders continues at schools such as Sandhurst in Britain and West Point in the USA.

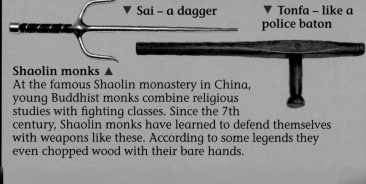

▼ Sai – a dagger   ▼ Tonfa – like a police baton

Shaolin monks ▲
At the famous Shaolin monastery in China, young Buddhist monks combine religious studies with fighting classes. Since the 7th century, Shaolin monks have learned to defend themselves with weapons like these. According to some legends they even chopped wood with their bare hands.

In the Shadow
of a Pyramid

Painful lessons
Egyptian teachers had a cruel slogan: "The ear of a boy is on his back, for he listens only when he is beaten." Copying this taught students their hieroglyphs – and reminded them that slackers would soon feel hippopotamus-skin lashes on their shoulders.

I N ANCIENT EGYPT'S SIZZLING climate, learning was a sweaty business, so school began early in the morning. Classes were tough and dull. By chanting and dreary exercises, boys learned Egypt's two different ways of writing. Each had hundreds of picture-signs. Mistakes earned a whipping, but success was rewarded. Good pupils became scribes – officials who used their reading and writing skills to help to run the country.

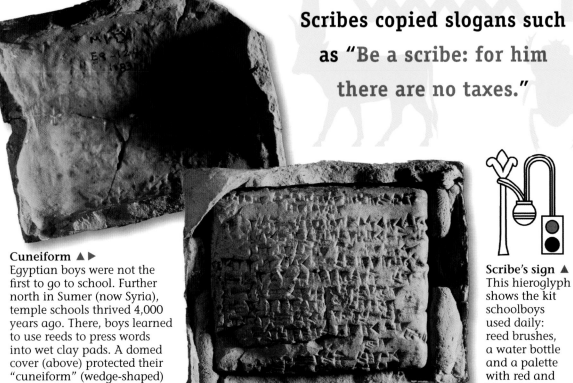

Scribes copied slogans such as "Be a scribe: for him there are no taxes."

Cuneiform ▲ ▶
Egyptian boys were not the first to go to school. Further north in Sumer (now Syria), temple schools thrived 4,000 years ago. There, boys learned to use reeds to press words into wet clay pads. A domed cover (above) protected their "cuneiform" (wedge-shaped) writing, like an envelope.

Scribe's sign ▲
This hieroglyph shows the kit schoolboys used daily: reed brushes, a water bottle and a palette with red and black ink.

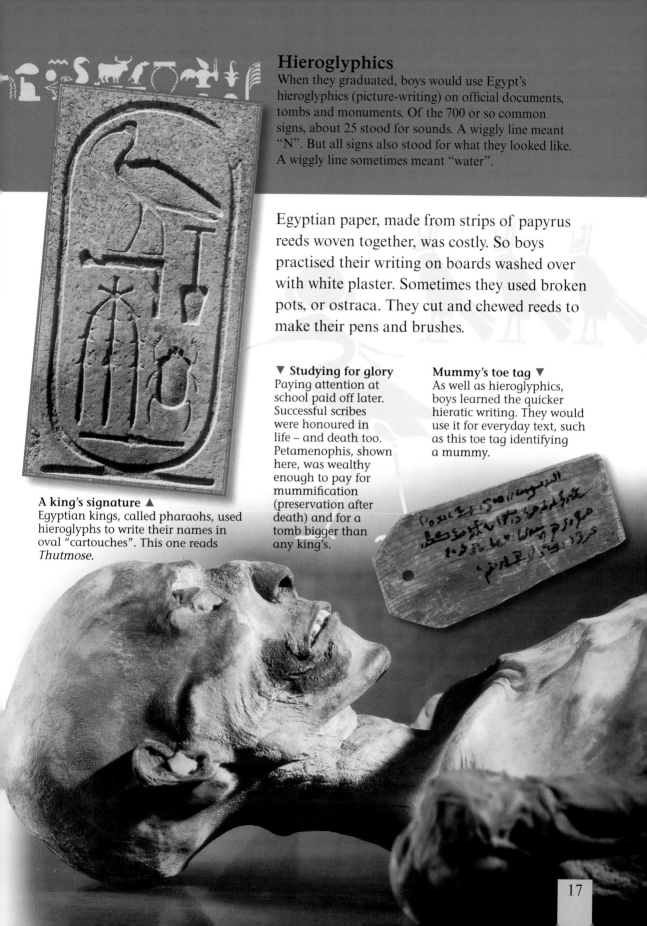

Hieroglyphics

When they graduated, boys would use Egypt's hieroglyphics (picture-writing) on official documents, tombs and monuments. Of the 700 or so common signs, about 25 stood for sounds. A wiggly line meant "N". But all signs also stood for what they looked like. A wiggly line sometimes meant "water".

Egyptian paper, made from strips of papyrus reeds woven together, was costly. So boys practised their writing on boards washed over with white plaster. Sometimes they used broken pots, or ostraca. They cut and chewed reeds to make their pens and brushes.

▼ Studying for glory
Paying attention at school paid off later. Successful scribes were honoured in life – and death too. Petamenophis, shown here, was wealthy enough to pay for mummification (preservation after death) and for a tomb bigger than any king's.

Mummy's toe tag ▼
As well as hieroglyphics, boys learned the quicker hieratic writing. They would use it for everyday text, such as this toe tag identifying a mummy.

A king's signature ▲
Egyptian kings, called pharaohs, used hieroglyphs to write their names in oval "cartouches". This one reads *Thutmose*.

Reasonable Chastisement

Paying a fine ▼
Naughty medieval students were often punished with fines. An Oxford college fined boys more who stayed out late, than boys who fired arrows at a tutor.

Medieval silver pennies ▶

FINES, LINES, SHAME AND pain all have the same aims in the schoolroom: to make lazy pupils study and to punish naughty ones. Until very recently, teachers could beat children to make them behave – as long as they used only "reasonable chastisement (punishment)". Further back in the past, there were fewer limits.

Ancient Egyptian, Greek and Roman children all felt the lash across their shoulders. In Rome, the expression "to hold out the hand for the cane" was another way of saying "to study". One Roman writer said that he would rather die than be a schoolboy again.

Would You Believe . . . ?

Not so reasonable
The law allowing only "reasonable" beatings began in 1860 when teacher Tom Hopley whipped "obstinate" Reginald Cancellor to death – for getting his multiplication tables wrong. Former pupils said he was a man of "utmost kindness and affection"!

School for apes ▼
Many artists drew beatings to make it clear that the picture showed a school. A 14th-century monk drew this scene of a school in the margin of a book he was copying. He drew the people as apes.

Bread and water ▲
In the early 16th century, teachers at French college Montaigu punished pupils who committed minor crimes by feeding them only bread and water. For fighting, young boys were beaten. Older boys got away with fines. A century later, whipping had replaced most punishments, even for students as old as 20.

"More wine, you bad boy"

With time, teachers grew more inventive about discipline. Medieval pupils were still beaten, but a few were lucky enough to get more gentle punishments. One Paris college had a prison cell to lock up pupils, and naughty German students were forced to buy their whole class wine or beer.

Inca teachers in Peru punished pupils by beating the soles of their feet, a torture now known as bastinado

Naming and shaming ▼
Separating out naughty pupils to shame them is a traditional punishment. In the past, a "dunce's cap" made the humiliation worse. So-called ignorant people were called dunces after 13th-century Scots thinker John Duns Scotus, whose ideas many people found baffling.

" HARD LINES ! "

18/2

Writing lines ▲
Writing lines, usually about what they have done wrong, keeps children from more enjoyable things and also provides valuable handwriting practice.

The threat of a beating controlled most classes, so schools often pinned up a menu of punishment. An 18th-century English school's menu of lashes was: lateness, 3; stealing, 9; missing church, 20. Truants suffered "the hissing and scoffing of ye whole school" – and 12 lashes.

No more canes

Opposition to beatings began more than 200 years ago. However, this was still one of the most common forms of punishment in Britain and the USA until the late 20th century. Today, more than 100 countries have banned beating, and pupils need no longer fear the "whoosh" of a cane.

Learning to Read and Write

Puzzling ring ▼
Turning learning into a game doesn't always make it easier! It's unlikely that this early 20th-century board made learning to read any quicker than books.

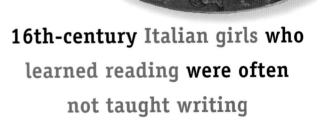

MASTERING THE alphabet is a challenge that every child struggles to overcome. But learning the 26 letters of the modern Latin alphabet – A to Z – is easy compared to learning to read and write eastern Asian languages. Japanese children must learn three ways of writing – and one has more than 11,000 different characters!

Today, the ability to read is a vital skill. Yet for much of history, only the very rich bothered with reading because books were scarce. They learned from hornbooks and hand-written Bibles or prayer books. The few libraries that existed kept their precious books on chains.

16th-century Italian girls who learned reading were often not taught writing

● ● ● ● ● ● ● ● ● ● ● ●

◄ **Eating the alphabet**
In the 1st century CE, Roman mothers helped their children to read by cutting cakes into the shapes of the alphabet. Hungry Italian children learned the same way in the 16th century, and alphabet sweets continue today.

歓
迎

Kanji characters
meaning "welcome"

◀ **Writing in Japan**
The beautiful characters of
Japanese Kanji writing are
tough to learn: there
are 900 characters.
But Katakana, the
46 sound-signs that
kids learn first, is
easier to write
than English.

Printing

When printing was
invented in the 15th
century, there were more
books but they were still
very expensive. Books only got
cheap enough to give to children
in the 19th century, when steam
power cut paper and printing
costs. Even then, not everyone
learned their letters: it wasn't
until the mid 20th century
that most people in England
learned to read and write.

Modern hornbooks ▼
Reading aloud still
helps kids to learn.
These children in
Senegal, Africa, are
using word boards
that have hardly
changed from the
medieval hornbook.

The First European Schools

▲ Printed books
The invention of printing around 1440 made books much cheaper and more common, and made learning to read easier. However, some four centuries would pass before books were cheap enough to give to every child in a schoolroom.

THE WORLD WAS CHANGING FAST in the 16th century. In Europe, followers of Christianity split into Protestants and Catholics, and churches and monasteries lost control of schools they had been running for centuries. New "grammar" schools sprung up – many of them free to students – aiming to teach Latin and Greek. Gradually, lessons began to cover more of the subjects we learn about now.

Martin Luther ▶
German monk Martin Luther did more than anyone else to shake up 16th-century education. To make reading the Bible easier, he translated it from Latin into German (right). By challenging the Pope, he divided Christians. His followers, the Protestants, took power and wealth away from the Church and made education less religious.

Would You Believe . . . ? Would You Believe . . . ?

Light reading
Studying was hard work in the 17th century. One educator suggested that pupils aged nine or ten should carry around in their pockets copies of religious books written in Latin. He thought this would give them something entertaining to read between their lessons!

◀ Vagabond students
In the 16th century, children of the poor, such as the Swiss scholar and writer Thomas Platter, travelled together in bands to colleges in distant towns. The youngest of these vagabond scholars made money by begging, stealing and singing in the street, paying it to older boys for protection. Penniless, Platter stole geese and slept in graveyards while studying.

Going to a lecture around 1350 ▶

◀ European universities
European universities
The youngest pupils at the first European universities had barely entered their teens, so the colleges were much more like schools than today's universities. Fines and beatings for misbehaviour were common.

◀ **Paris University in the 14th century**

European swords from the 17th century

Colleges that students attended were very different from today's. They were rough and had strict rules and stricter punishments. Unless they were from rich families, pupils had to work, steal or beg to eat and study.

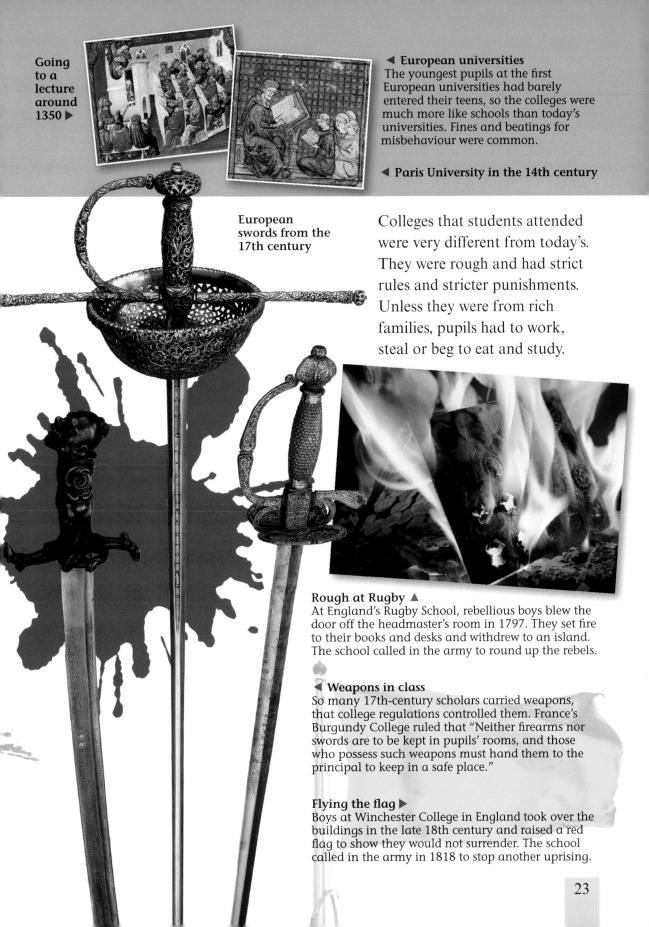

Rough at Rugby ▲
At England's Rugby School, rebellious boys blew the door off the headmaster's room in 1797. They set fire to their books and desks and withdrew to an island. The school called in the army to round up the rebels.

◀ **Weapons in class**
So many 17th-century scholars carried weapons, that college regulations controlled them. France's Burgundy College ruled that "Neither firearms nor swords are to be kept in pupils' rooms, and those who possess such weapons must hand them to the principal to keep in a safe place."

Flying the flag ▶
Boys at Winchester College in England took over the buildings in the late 18th century and raised a red flag to show they would not surrender. The school called in the army in 1818 to stop another uprising.

In the Schoolyard

Would You Believe . . . ?

Deadly games
Playing at war sometimes turned into the real thing. In spring 1400, thousands of London children chose two "kings" and fought a battle under their command "with their utmost strength, whereby many died, struck with blows or trampled underfoot".

PULSING WITH ENERGY, life and competition, a school playground is a place to share secrets, let off steam or just play. Schoolyard games are as ancient as school itself. Among the oldest are skill games such as throwing balls, skipping and jacks. In ancient Rome, children played with nuts, and the phrase "when nuts are abandoned" meant "grown up".

Today's schoolyard games are quite different from those of adults, but it was not always like this. In Europe, in 1600, children aged three and older played adult games and even gambled for money.

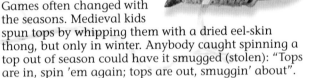

In a spin ▶
Games often changed with the seasons. Medieval kids spun tops by whipping them with a dried eel-skin thong, but only in winter. Anybody caught spinning a top out of season could have it smugged (stolen): "Tops are in, spin 'em again; tops are out, smuggin' about".

Adults once played children's games, too. A picture from a 14th-century book shows them playing frog in the middle.

Marbles ▶
Children have played with glass marbles only since about 1850. Previously, rich children's marbles were made of stone (real marble gave them their modern name); poor kids made do with pottery. Whatever the material, though, the games were the same.

◀ **Cockfighting**
On Shrove Tuesday (Pancake Day) in 12th-century London, it was a tradition that "all the schoolchildren brought their fighting cocks to their master". Cockerels need no encouragement to fight each other. Betting on the winner was hugely popular – even in the playground.

Beetle mania ▼
Some games ended because they were cruel to animals. But in the past, children did not care. In ancient Rome, they harnessed tiny carts to mice. In ancient Egypt and medieval Europe, they tied thread to beetles and made them fly in circles.

Copying adults

Games sometimes help to prepare children for life after school. Boys' endless playground battles are a reminder that, until recently, warfare was always part of adult lives. And before women had careers, girls acted out in games the jobs they would later do for real as wives and mothers.

◄ **Board and pebbles**
The children playing this African game of mancala are using a special board, but they don't really need one. Anyone can play the game with fruit-pips, pebbles or shells, and a few chalk lines.

Boarding Schools

Hoplite said to be Leonidas, King of Sparta

FOR THE FULL-ON EDUCATION experience, nothing comes close to a boarding school. Real-life Hogwarts don't teach witches and wizards, but they do give their pupils a home, a giant family and a special, 24/7 education. Boarding schools began in Europe: there was a tradition there of sending children away to study. By the mid 18th century, every English or French small town had one or two boarding schools.

▲ **Military boarder**
In the 6th century BCE, Spartan schools in Greece trained young hoplites (armed warriors). To toughen the boys, they were starved. Pupils found stealing food were beaten – not for theft but for getting caught.

▲ **Gurukul**
In traditional gurukul schools in India, pupils lived with the guru, a Hindu tutor, often in forests far from their homes. They did household chores for the guru, including cleaning, laundry and cooking.

Would You Believe . . . . ?
Fatal schools
Even the very best schools "lost" pupils. At France's Saint-Cyr school (see "Murderous Pupils" opposite), only the daughters of noble people in the army boarded, yet one in six girls graduated in coffins. Slaves and slum children were less likely to die than pupils at Saint-Cyr.

In 19th-century Britain, harsh charity boarding schools taught orphans – and often starved and killed them too. Better schools educated the sons of government officials who were abroad running the country's distant empire.

Removing lice ▶
Fleas, bedbugs and head lice spread quickly among children packed together in boarding schools. However, children who attended day schools were often just as lousy.

Murderous pupils

Most pupils in even the worst boarding schools put up with dreadful food, brutal teachers and freezing classrooms, but some struck back. An 18th-century French school, the *Maison Royale de Saint-Cyr*, Paris, expelled three girls for attempted murder. They twice tried to kill one of the teachers they hated by putting hemlock in her soup and salad.

Hemlock flowers

An 18th-century writer thought that boarding-school girls had bad health because they had to share a bed

▲ Charity farm

Conditions in British 18th-century charity boarding schools were terrible. An inspector reported hungry children wearing rags and sharing their rooms with pigs, chickens and turkeys. It's not surprising that he added, "The children did not appear cheerful."

Dickensian squalor ▶

For his 1839 book *Nicholas Nickleby*, English author Charles Dickens invented Dotheboys Hall, a boarding school run by a cruel teacher. One of the boys is Smike, shown here in a play of the book. Dickens based the school on conditions common in real schools.

27

Special and Unusual Schools

▲ **Gladiator school**
Ancient Rome's *ludi* were special schools for gladiators. These professional warriors, usually slaves, battled to the death in the city's colossal stadium. In training, they used harmless wooden swords.

I F YOU WERE PLUCKED FROM YOUR classroom and dropped in another one in a distant land, you would soon learn to fit in because most schools share the same pattern of lessons, books and breaks. A few, though, are different. They teach smart kids or those with special abilities in things such as music, dance, sport – or crime!

Would You Believe . . . ?

Sea school
Graduates from crime schools in 19th-century New York moved to a different kind of education if they got caught. In 1869, the city bought a sailing ship. They put on board 250 "wild, reckless and semi-criminal lads" who spent the next six months learning to be sailors.

As long ago as the 7th century, Chinese teachers picked out clever scholars to study in the emperor's school. "Gifted and talented" classes continue today.

Schools of villainy ▶
In 19th-century London, villains ran pickpocket schools for street urchins with nimble fingers. In typical classes, students learned first on tailors' dummies, then on teachers, before being let loose on the public.

Two pickpockets with a victim

◀ **Steiner schools**
At these unusual primary schools, traditional skills like writing and arithmetic take second place. Teachers instead develop imagination and general knowledge. Students may not start to learn to read until age seven.

● **The school on Papa Stour island in Scotland, UK, closed in 2003 when both pupils stayed at home**

Performing arts ▼
Students at special schools, such as these girls at a performing arts school in Phnom Penh, Cambodia, do not escape regular lessons. They do ordinary studies too, and have a long, tiring school day.

Schools that bring together children with similar interests are rather like apprenticeships of the past, where master craftsmen taught the secrets of their trade. Because learning is easier the sooner it begins, children as young as six may study full-time, but more begin with summer schools.

Revolution in the Classroom

Back to nature ▼
French leader Louis Saint Just wanted children to leave home aged five, sleep on mats and live on fruit, vegetables, bread and water.

WHEN A NATION'S PEOPLE rise up and grab political power during a revolution, they want change for themselves – and their children. Schools come near the top of their wish-list. Revolutionaries can't resist "improving" education and ridding it of old traditions. One leader of the American Revolution, Benjamin Rush, said schools should turn children into "republican machines".

Rather than raising a new race of robots, Rush wanted to teach children about their new country, so that they would rule it wisely. After a lot of discussion, America's leaders agreed to leave each state to decide how to run their own schools.

◀ The guillotine came to stand for the French Revolution.

French Revolution ▶
Priests, monks and nuns taught French children until 1789. Then ordinary people seized power from the wealthy few and destroyed religious schools. They eventually provided a better education for children.

Would You Believe...?

Educating the emperor
China's 1911 revolution left one school unchanged. It was in a palace in Beijing and it had only one pupil: Puyi, the six-year-old emperor. He was treated like a god and taught by a Scotsman until 1924, when he was thrown out by a jealous general.

A French revolutionary suggested that to graduate from school at 16, students should have to swim across a river

A Chairman Mao badge from the Cultural Revolution ▶

Cultural Revolution ▲
Communist Mao Zedong led a second Chinese revolt in 1966. The Cultural Revolution tore China apart. Students and teachers were forced to farm.

Out with Confucius ▲
Before 1949, Chinese children learned to respect the emperor, and studied the work of Confucius – a Chinese thinker of the 6th century BCE.

The Chinese revolution of 1949 swept away thousands of years of tradition. The country's new leaders hurried to teach children freedom, equality and brotherhood – and to give them practical skills to modernise the world's largest nation.

Red revolution

Following Russia's communist revolution of 1917, the government threw out books with "outdated" ideas – leaving schools with no books! Americans claimed "Reds are ruining children of Russia", but 40 years on they would come to admire Russian schools.

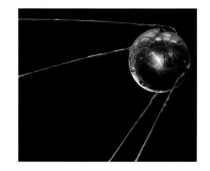

Space first ▲
In 1957, Russians launched the satellite *Sputnik*. Shocked at being beaten into space, Americans began to ask whether Russians could teach them a thing or two about technology education.

Teaching Girls?
Ridiculous!

"**A** GIRL SHOULD LEARN to sew and not to read unless you want to make her a nun." This saying from medieval Italy explains why so few girls went to school. Studying might have helped a son to succeed, but for a daughter it was a disadvantage. Men wanted their wives to be sweet, obedient, pretty – but not educated, please!

In 1792, English feminist Mary Wollstonecraft was one of the first to suggest that girls should be educated like boys. She wrote, "Women are not inferior to men, but appear to be only because they lack education." Not everyone agreed: it was 50 years before colleges for women were common in Europe and the USA.

? Would You Believe . . . ? Would You Believe . . . ?

Tough lessons
Even great difficulties don't stop smart girls from learning. In an Italian convent in the Renaissance (1400–1600), girls were not allowed in the chapel but heard services through a grille. One learned to read by repeating letters spoken and signed by the chaplain.

SUFFRAGETTE SERIES N°

SUFFRAGETTE VOTE-GETTING
THE EASIEST WAY.

©COPYRIGHTED

Rights for women ▶
When women fought to be allowed to vote in their countries' elections, they also campaigned for girls to get the same educational chances as boys. These "suffragettes" didn't win their battle until 1920 in the USA and ten years later in Britain. On this poster, a cartoonist makes fun of the campaign.

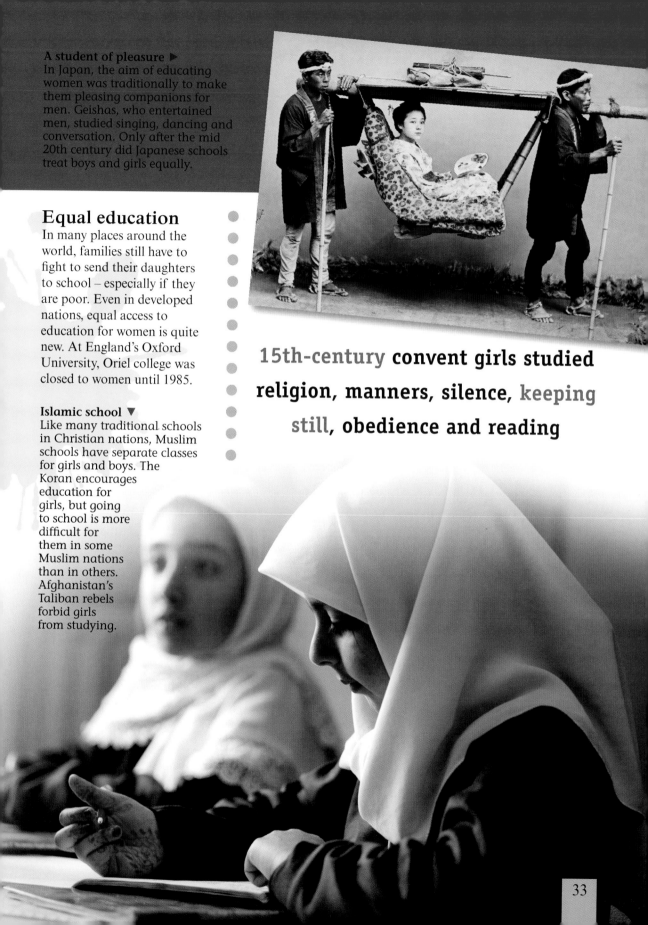

A student of pleasure ▷
In Japan, the aim of educating women was traditionally to make them pleasing companions for men. Geishas, who entertained men, studied singing, dancing and conversation. Only after the mid 20th century did Japanese schools treat boys and girls equally.

Equal education

In many places around the world, families still have to fight to send their daughters to school – especially if they are poor. Even in developed nations, equal access to education for women is quite new. At England's Oxford University, Oriel college was closed to women until 1985.

Islamic school ▼
Like many traditional schools in Christian nations, Muslim schools have separate classes for girls and boys. The Koran encourages education for girls, but going to school is more difficult for them in some Muslim nations than in others. Afghanistan's Taliban rebels forbid girls from studying.

15th-century convent girls studied religion, manners, silence, keeping still, obedience and reading

33

All Work and
no Education

COMPARED TO SITTING in a classroom, harvesting a field of golden wheat sounds like a holiday. But if instead of school you had to climb up inside a sooty, scorching chimney every day, which would you pick? Millions of children, past and present, have never had the choice. They have had to work to eat.

The idea that all children should study is surprisingly new. In the past, only those who expected to work with their brains got education. Most people earned money using their muscles so, as children, they never went to school.

Coal miners ▲
In 1911, these "breaker boys" from Pennsylvania, USA, could not go to school during the day because they sorted coal at a mine. Children continued to work in American industry until this was made illegal in 1938.

Chimney sweeps ▶
19th-century chimney sweeps drove nimble boys up chimneys to clean soot that no brush could reach. Many died of falls or suffocation. When England's parliament banned this in 1840, more of these "climbing boys" could study. But deaths continued for another 35 years.

Would You Believe . . . ? Would You Believe . . . ?

That's education?
English factory kids got lucky in 1833. New laws cut their work to 54 hours a week. They also had to have two hours' schooling each day. However, many factory "teachers" knew less than their pupils. They signed the register with a cross because they couldn't write.

The USA passed the first "education for all" laws in 1642, but 300 years passed before they were obeyed

Rich pupils ▶

As early as the 17th century, towns in Scotland had to make free schooling available by law. But only children of wealthy families attended. The poor needed their children's wages and kept them out of school.

In the 18th century, people beg accept that everyone had the ri an education – not just the rich. wasn't until 1891 that education came in Britain. In the USA, ed was made free for children only i

Making clothes ▼

In Bangladesh, many children cannot go to school because they work in the fields or, like this boy, in a factory. Primary education is free, but many parents cannot afford paper, pens and the fares to school.

Kept out of sc

There's enough time i day for children to stu work. However, 200 mi children worldwide wor long hours that they ca go to school. Many are more than slaves and are forced to do dangerous t

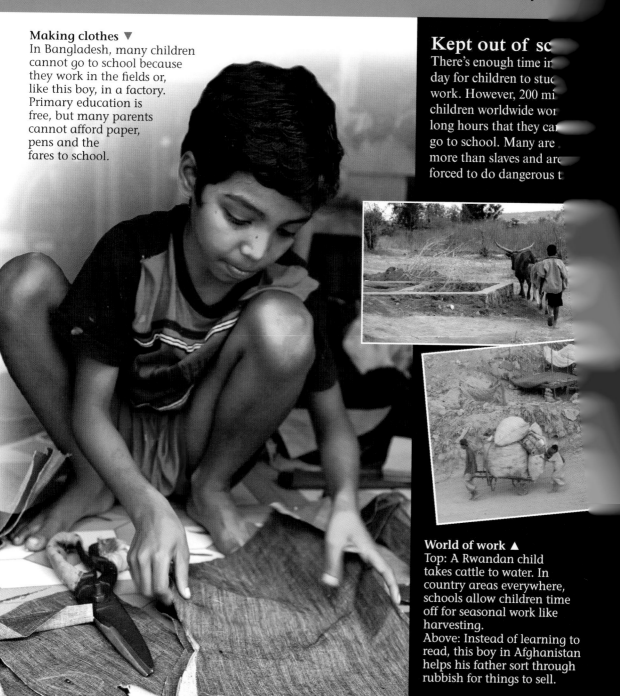

World of work ▲

Top: A Rwandan child takes cattle to water. In country areas everywhere, schools allow children time off for seasonal work like harvesting.
Above: Instead of learning to read, this boy in Afghanistan helps his father sort through rubbish for things to sell.

One-room Schoolhouse

IN A CLASS OF A ONE-ROOM SCHOOL the smallest pupils could barely see over their desks – and the oldest could hardly fit into them. Schools like this were once common outside cities. In them, children from reception to graduation shared one teacher. Often her job included lighting fires, cooking and cleaning as well as teaching.

▲ **In the classroom**
Six poor children studied in this schoolhouse in 19th-century Sussex, England. The only teaching aids were a globe and an abacus, but the class was lucky – most villages had no free school at the time.

Schoolhouse of the Masai people in East Africa

◀ ▲ ▼ **Around the world**
Where one-room schoolhouses are still in use, they are usually built from local materials and look very like the village homes from which their pupils come. Often, the children's parents built the school themselves, on a patch of land given by one of them, using materials they donated.

In most areas of the world, one-room schoolhouses began to fall out of use in the mid 20th century. Buses took pupils to bigger schools that served several villages and had separate classes for each age group. However, one-room schools have not disappeared completely. In some isolated communities, this traditional type of education continues.

Schoolhouse of an Amish community in Pennsylvania, USA

▼ French one-room school

The 2002 film *To Be and to Have* follows teacher Georges Lopez in a one-room school in Saint-Etienne-sur-Usson, France. His four- to ten-year-old pupils learn as quickly and as well as those in much bigger, better-funded schools.

▲ Alan Shepard

America's first man in space in 1961, Alan Shepard studied at a one-room schoolhouse in East Derry, New Hampshire. His teacher, Bertha Wiggins, taught six grades of pupils together, a task that required firm discipline. Shepard remembers that ... "She was about nine feet tall and ... always had the ruler ready to whack the knuckles if somebody got out of hand."

Nebraska schoolhouse ▼

A few one-room schoolhouses remain in use in the USA in remote country areas. These two girls from Nebraska ride their horses to school, leaving them to graze while they study in the room you can see behind them.

Would You Believe . . . ?

Heating the school
One-room schoolhouses in Irish country areas used to be heated with peat fires. The pupils themselves supplied the fuel – either they carried a block of peat to school with their books, or their father delivered a cart load at the beginning of the cold winter term.

Home Schooling

YOU CAN'T ESCAPE education but you can avoid school – if your parents teach you at home. Some parents do this because they don't approve of what their children learn in school, or they figure they could do a better job themselves. Some have no choice: the nearest school is just too far away.

In the past, children learning at home used regular school books, sometimes with help from two-way radio. Today, many parents use custom-made lesson plans nicknamed "school in a box". The internet also helps to keep learning up to date.

▼ Nazi ideas
The Nazi rulers of 1930s Germany saw schools as places to spread their ideas, and passed laws making all kids attend. Although pupils had to return all Nazi books in 1945 (below), the laws about school attendance have not changed. Parents who want to teach their kids at home have to move abroad.

▲ **Home schooling was normal in 19th-century families**

Some kids learning by radio in Australia had no electricity so they had to pedal generators to power their radios

Home schooling isn't for everyone. Parents who do it must be well educated. Children can miss out on things that only a school can provide, such as making friends quickly and having a sense of belonging that comes from being in a big group.

Hard home work
Studying at home may sound like fun, but it's no easier than regular school. Countries that permit home schooling usually keep a tight check on what parents teach. Those that break the rules face penalties or even jail.

▲ **Learning by radio**
Children from remote Australian farms used to go to boarding school or they received and returned assignments by post. But in the 1950s, the School of the Air began broadcasting lessons to pupils. Students and their teachers linked up with two-way radio.

▲ **Making a choice**
In the USA, the country's laws do not permit prayer or the reading of the Bible or Koran in classes at the free, tax-funded public schools. Many religious parents therefore choose to educate their children at home.

Success without Schooling

EDUCATION IS WHAT'S LEFT when you've forgotten everything you learned in the classroom, according to science genius Albert Einstein. He made amazing discoveries in spite of what he learned at school. Einstein wasn't alone. As the examples on this page show, you don't *have* to finish school to succeed.

◄ **A bright spark**
The inventor of recorded music (1877) and lightbulbs (1879), Thomas Edison said he was "always at the foot of the class". His mother withdrew him from school after his teacher said his brain was scrambled.

◄ **Henry Ford**
American Henry Ford was a mechanical wizard and was repairing watches by the time he was 15. He left school the following year to work on a factory metal-working machine. The famous motor company he started in 1903 was the first to mass-produce cars.

1907 Model-K Ford touring car

Abraham Lincoln ▶
The 16th US president, shown here on a US 1-cent coin, had just a few months at school in 1815. But he read every book he could get his hands on. This led his father to call Lincoln lazy!

The stamp of genius ▲
German physicist Albert Einstein is everyone's idea of a genius. At school he felt stifled by memorising facts and used a doctor's note to escape. He then failed the entrance exam of the college to which he applied. He devised his famous Special Theory of Relativity in 1905, while working as a young clerk in a patent office.

It was not dropping out of school that made these people so successful. They were highly intelligent and original thinkers. Some were so bright that school simply bored them. Other people had to quit school and were forced to take jobs to support their families.

Too cool for school

Think carefully before declaring yourself a genius and bunking off for a week – or forever. Today, it's more difficult to succeed without schooling than it was in the past. Employers are more picky about diplomas and certificates. "I'm a genius" may have worked for Einstein, but it may not work for you!

SpaceShipOne ▲
Riding in a piggy-back rocket like this one, the first space tourists will have tickets bought from Richard Branson. Branson left school at 15 but is one of Britain's most successful businessmen.

Would You Believe . . . ?

Bill Gates
Perhaps the most famous dropout of all is Microsoft founder Bill Gates, who never finished his degree at Harvard University, dropping out in 1977. But Gates was brilliant at school, where he reprogrammed the school computer to make sure he was in classes with the most girls.

"I have never let schooling interfere with my education." So said author Mark Twain.

Testing Times

EXAMINATIONS and tests are a tedious part of every school year, but it wasn't always like this. When Socrates taught in ancient Greece, some 2,500 years ago, there were no tests, only conversations. If pupils' answers to Socrates's questions showed they did not understand a lesson, the philosopher just carried on teaching until everyone in the class understood.

Would You Believe . . . ? Would You Believe . . . ?

That's very difficult
During the Ming dynasty in China, 650 to 350 years ago, exams for would-be government officials were the longest-running tests in history – and the hardest. About 10,000 people took the exam each year, and only one or two passed at the highest level!

Testing began in China – at work, not in schools. In the 22nd century BCE, Emperor Shun set examinations for public officials. Those who passed were promoted. The rest were fired. Educational testing began hundreds of years later, in 1219, with written exams at Italy's Bologna University.

Bottom marks

Schoolchildren didn't face exams until 1894, when schools in Boston, USA, introduced them. Anxious to compare schools, the city's education committee set all pupils written tests. The scores – just 35 percent in arithmetic – disappointed teachers.

◀ **The empress who loved exams**
In the 7th century, Wu Zetian, the only woman to rule China as an empress, made the government entry exams fairer, so that common people stood a better chance of becoming officials. One of the exams tested the ability to write poems.

Written tests were rare until cheap paper replaced costly parchment in the 12th century

Marble carving of a group of students from Bologna

▲ **Early tests**
Bologna University was one of the first universities and began testing law students in the 13th century. The tests included written essay questions and traditional verbal quizzes.

Today, parents, schools and universities rely on tests to check on students' learning progress and achievement. But given the choice, most pupils and many teachers would prefer the classes of Socrates, where there were no right or wrong answers.

● ● ● ● ● ● ● ● ● ●

◀ **US recruitment poster 1917**

TREAT'EM ROUGH!

JOIN THE TANKS
United States Tank Corps

OPEN TO FIGHTING MEN ALL CLASSES 18 to 45
Tenth Floor at 19 West 44th Street, New York City

▲ **War-time tests**
Multiple-choice tests were the invention of Kansas educator Frederick Kelly. He brought them in to check the knowledge of soldiers recruited to fight for the USA in World War I (1914–18). Ordinary tests with written answers were taking too long to mark, and the country needed the soldiers quickly.

▲ **Tests today**
Testing is big business. Just one American company tests three million pupils each year. It's controversial too. Some parents think exams just stress their kids and don't measure their real abilities.

What's so Weird about That?

IT'S A JUNGLE, A CASTLE, A CAVE or a shady tree. It's a place to study reading – or fighting, dancing, rhyming, finding food or how to avoid being bitten by a snake. It can start almost before you've learned to speak, or when you're already an adult. But school is not just about learning. It's also about finding out what it means to be you.

● ● ● ● ● ● ● ● ● ● ● ●

Make school your own

If your school life seems ordinary, then why not make it weirder, wackier – or wickeder? School is what you make of it. Remember the saying, "School days are the best days of your life!"

You may decide that school is the wrong place to find out about yourself. But for me, and for millions of others, it wasn't. School got me interested in everything, the weirder the better. It got me asking why? I never got tired of looking for the answer.

Would You Believe . . . . ? Would You Find Would You Believe . . . . ?

Teachers' Day
Many nations set aside a day each year to honour their teachers. In Taiwan, Teachers' Day ceremonies include the sacrifice of a cow, a pig and a goat. Students who pluck the pig's "hairs of wisdom" will be blessed with knowledge and good luck.

Walking to school ▲
When school's a routine, it's easy to take it for granted and forget how hard some children have to struggle to get an education. These orphans live with their grandfather in Zimbabwe. No teacher lives locally to their home, so each day they walk 7 km (4 miles) to the nearest school – and back again.

In ancient Rome, schoolchildren had a goddess, Minerva. The school year began on her festival day.

Find out More

You can find out lots more about the history of education from these websites and places to visit.

Websites

The Singing Playground
www.vam.ac.uk/vastatic/microsites/1513_
singing_playground
Listen to playground songs from around the world on this beautiful V&A Museum of Childhood site.

Student life
www.bbc.co.uk/schools/studentlife/schoolissues
This BBC *Student Life* website has pages on home schooling and bullying.

School trip
www.bbc.co.uk/schools/studentlife/games/
crashcourse/index.shtml
Create a comic about a school trip to Greece.

Victorian children at school, work and play
www.bbc.co.uk/schools/Victorians/standard/school
Suitable for younger children, this BBC site looks at 19th-century school life.

UNICEF
www.unicef.org/voy/explore/education/explore_
education.php
Check out Brain Teasers and Photo Journal on these web pages from the United Nations Children's Fund.

Places to visit

Alnwick Castle
Alnwick
Northumberland, NE66 1NQ
Telephone: 01665 510777
Website: www.alnwickcastle.com/thingstosee_
detail.php?item=4
Study as a page or squire at the castle. You'll fire a trebuchet, learn sword-fighting and jousting, and brave the dreaded garderobe!

Prehistoric Gower Experience
Dryad Bushcraft
53 Woodcote
Killay
Swansea, SA2 7AY
Telephone: 01792 547213
Website: www.dryadbushcraft.co.uk/courses/
prehistoric_gower_experience.html
This outdoor learning centre teaches the skills and crafts that children had to master to survive in Neolithic Gower, Wales. These include flint tool making, foraging on the seashore, building shelters, making fire, tracking and willow craft.

The Ragged School Museum
40-50 Copperfield Road,
London, E3 4RR
Telephone: 020 8980 6405
Website: www.raggedschoolmuseum.org.uk
The Ragged School gives you an authentic glimpse of school, work and home life in Victorian East London. Take part in a lesson with slate boards, easels and even dunces' hats. Learn more about the work of Dr Barnardo, who set up this free school in the 19th century.

Scotland Street School
225 Scotland Street
Glasgow, G5 8QB
Telephone: 0141 287 0500
Website: www.glasgowmuseums.com/venue/
index.cfm?venueid=12
Witness the changing face of Scottish schoolrooms from the Victorian era through to the 50s and 60s. Listen to and read about students' memories over time. Have a look for your family's old school photographs or follow the interpretation and activity trail around the school.

Hawkshead Grammar School Museum
Hawkshead
Cumbria, LA22 0NT
Telephone: 01539 436735
Website: www.hawksheadgrammar.org.uk
The museum in this old grammar school building houses a unique collection of artefacts relating to the ancient school, some of which date back to the 16th century.

Glossary

Did you read anything you didn't understand? Some of the more complicated and unusual terms used in this book are explained here.

abacus
Simple counting frame, usually made of beads sliding on rods.

Amish
American Christians who live in communities that lead simple lives, rejecting modern conveniences.

archaeologist
Scientist who learns about the past by digging up artefacts (objects made by past people).

Aztecs
Native Central American people who ruled Mexico between the 14th and 16th centuries.

cartouche
Ancient Egyptian way of writing a king's name inside a frame.

cuneiform
Method of writing with wedge-shaped marks in soft clay, used by the people of Sumer (now Iraq) 5,000 years ago.

empire
Large region ruled by a group of people under an emperor.

feminist
Anyone who believes that women are the equals of men and should be treated as such.

guru
Teacher, especially of the Hindu religion.

hieroglyph
Word- or sound-sign in a system of picture-writing.

Incas
People of South America who ruled Peru and Chile from about 1200 to 1533.

Kanji
Japanese picture-writing system with thousands of characters.

Katakana
Writing system of 46 sound-signs used in Japan.

medieval
From the Middle Ages, a 1,000-year period of European history starting in the 5th century CE.

monastery
Home and place of work and worship for monks (men devoted to God).

mosque
Place of worship for Muslims, followers of the Islamic religion.

Nazis
National Socialists: members of the party that ruled Germany between 1933 and 1945.

parchment
Writing material made of calf skin, which was used in Europe instead of paper until the 12th century.

philosopher
Anyone who thinks deeply and seeks the truth.

Reds
Nickname for Russian and other communists – people who believe in the fair distribution of wealth and equal opportunities.

Renaissance
300-year period of experiment, learning and rediscovery of ancient knowledge that began in 14th-century Italy.

revolution
Social change, often violent, in which people seize political power from their rulers.

Sparta
Warrior city-state of southern Greece that ruled the region around the Eurotas river from the 7th to 4th century BCE.

Stone Age
The time, before written history began, when people used stone tools and weapons.

suffragette
Woman who fought for suffrage (the right to vote in political elections).

Taliban
Military group of strict followers of the Islamic religion, who ruled Afghanistan from 1996 to 2001.

Vikings
Scandinavian seafaring people who raided European ships and coasts in the 8th to 11th centuries.

Index

Picture credits
The publisher would like to thank the following for their kind permission to reproduce their photographs:

Position key: c=centre; b=bottom; l=left; r=right; t=top

Front cover image: Hemera

4c: Ainaco/Corbis; 5tr: Matthew Scherf/iStockphoto; 5r: Heritage Image Partnership; 6bl: Martin Shields/Science Photo Library; 7t: Mary Evans/Asia Media; 7br: iStockphoto; 7bc: Chris Hutchison/iStockphoto; 8cl: The Art Archive/National Archaelogical Museum Athens/Gianni Dagli Orti; 8tc: Simon Spoon/iStockphoto; 8br: Heritage Image Partnership; 9tr: The Art Archive/Archaelogical Museum Saintes/Gianni Dagli Orti; 10tr: York Archaeological Trust for Excavation and Research Ltd.; 11l: Heritage Image Partnership/The Board of Trustees of the Armouries; 12bl: Jodi Jacobson/iStockphoto; 13c: Occidor Ltd/Robert Harding; 13tr: Heritage Image Partnership; 14cr: The Art Archive/Prehistoric Museum Moesgard Hojbjerg Denmark/Gianni Dagli Orti; 14tr: Simon Spoon/iStockphoto; 15t: Ricardo Funari/BrazilPhotos/Alamy; 15cl: Heritage Image Partnership; 15br: Gunnar Eden/iStockphoto; 16bl: The Art Archive/Corbis; 17cl: iStockphoto; 17b: Giani Dagli Orti/Corbis; 17cr: Birmingham Museums & Art Gallery; 18bl: The British Library; 18c: Stanislav Khalamenkov/iStockphoto; 18tr: Martin McCarthy/iStockphoto; 18cl: iStockphoto; 18c: Gene Krebs/iStockphoto; 19bl: World History Archive/Alamy; 19tr: Mary Evans Picture Library; 20cl: Glenda Powers/iStockphoto; 20bc: Dan Chippendale/iStockphoto; 20cr: Birmingham Museums & Art Gallery; 21b: Phillipe Lissac/Godong/Corbis; 21tl: JunjiTakemoto/iStockphoto; 22c: James

L. Amos/Corbis; 23cr: Rick Hinson/iStockphoto; 23br: iStockphoto; 23cl: Heritage Image Partnership; 24bl: Syad Lan Sabawoon/epa/Corbis; 24cr: Ivonne Wierink-vanWetten/iStockphoto; 25cl: Erik Koistad/iStockphoto; 25bl: Alf Ertsland/iStockphoto; 26br: Sheila Terry/Science Photo Library; 26cl: Indiapicture/Alamy; 27cl: Photodisc/OUP; 27tr: Peter Clark/iStockphoto; 27cr: Paul Doyle/Lebrecht Music & Arts; 27tl: David Foreman/iStockphoto; 28br: Heritage Image Partnership; 29b: LOOK Die Bildagentur der Fotografen GmbH/Alamy; 29tl: Colin McPherson/Corbis; 30br: The Gallery Collection/Corbis; 30cr: Juan Monino/iStockphoto; 30cr: Dan Chippendale/iStockphoto; 30tr: Drew Hadley/iStockphoto; 31br: NASA; 31tl: Mary Evans Picture Library; 31cr: Hannes Nimpuno/iStockphoto; 32br: Rykoff Collection/Corbis; 33tr: Stapleton Collection/Corbis; 33b: Andrew Fox/Corbis; 34bc: Rykoff Collection/Corbis; 34tl: Corbis; 35cr: iStockphoto; 35br: Danish Khan/iStockphoto; 35bl: Andrew Holbrooke/Corbis; 36tr: Richard Platt; 36br: Birmingham Museums; 36cr: Eliza Snow/iStockphoto; 36cl: Wolfgang Kaehler/Alamy; 37tl: The Kobal Collection; 37tr: NASA; 37b: Annie Griffiths Belt/Corbis; 38b: Bettmann/Corbis; 39cr: Yvonne Chamberlain/iStockphoto; 39t: Patrick Ward/Corbis; 40b: Car Culture/Corbis; 41c: Ryan Mulhall/iStockphoto; 41tr tc: Peter Spiro/iStockphoto; 42tr: iStockphoto; 42bl: Heritage Image Partnership/The Board of Trustees of the Armouries; 43tr: Visual Arts Library (London)/Alamy; 43cl: Swim Inc 2, LLC/Corbis; 43br: iStockphoto; 44c: Gideon Mendel/Corbis

Every effort has been made to trace the copyright holders of images. The publishers apologise for any omissions.

Quotation from Alan Shepard on page 37 by kind permission of the Academy of Achievement, Washington D.C., USA.